A SKETCH OF THE HISTORY OF CUTCH

A SKETCH OF THE HISTORY OF CUTCH

JAMES BURNS

GYAN

Published by

Gyan Publishing House
5, Ansari Road
Daryaganj, New Delhi-110002
Phone: 011-47034999, 9811692060
E-mail: books@gyanbooks.com

Distribution Network
gyanbooks.com
India, USA, Canada, UK, Australia, France

ISBN : 978-81-212-4021-5 (PB)
First Published, Edinburgh, 1839

2nd Impression 2020

Printed at: Gyan Press, Delhi.

A Sketch of the History of Cutch
Author: James Burns

PRELIMINARY NOTICE.

The following "Sketch of the History of Cutch since its connexion with the British Government" was compiled from public documents some years ago, as a supplement to a short history of that country by Captain Charles Walter, and in order to gratify the curiosity of a few friends, who expressed a strong desire to know something of the life and proceedings of the Ex-Rao, Bharmuljee, a state prisoner in Bhooj. Not having Captain Walter's papers to refer to, I have prefixed a short outline of the early history of Cutch, which consists simply of extracts from official reports by the Honourable Mountstuart Elphinstone, Colonel Henry Pottinger, political resident at Bhooj, and captain James Holland, deputy quarter-master general of the Bombay Army. A brief account of Cutch and its Inhabitants has also been inserted as an Introductory Chapter, although the subject has been almost exhausted by the late Captain M'Murdo and others.

The following Letter, which has reference to the Historical Sketch of Cutch, may be inserted here :—

Bombay Castle, 22d *April* 1830

(Political Department, No. 526.)

Sir,—I am directed to acknowledge the re ceipt of your letter, dated the 29th March, with a copy of one from Dr. Burnes, and to request that you will convey to that officer the thanks of government for the valuable sketch of the recent History of Cutch which accompanied it.

You will also be pleased to express to Dr. Burnes the real satisfaction with which government observes public officers devote their leisure to such objects of useful research, and to acquaint him that his clear and concise account of Cutch will be brought to the notice of the Honourable the Court of Directors.—I have the honour to be, &c.

(Signed) T. Williamson,
Secretary to Government.

SKETCH

OF THE

HISTORY OF CUTCH.

SECTION I.

OUTLINE OF THE HISTORY OF CUTCH BEFORE THE BRITISH CONNEXION.

About the ninth century of the Christian era, a body of supposed Moosulmans* of the Summa tribe emigrated from Sinde, and, under the guidance of five brothers, settled in Cutch, of which

* "Extraordinary as the fact may appear, it is stated in the Cutch annals, that these Summas were originally Mahommedans. Much doubt hangs over the early history of the Jharejahs, but they are generally understood to be a branch of the Jadoo Rajpoots, (children of the moon) descendants of Chrishud, who settled finally in the desert on the shore of Indus, under the appellation of Bhuttees and Sumaichas. The Bhuttees are well known as the Rajpoots of Jessulmeer, and there can be little reasonable doubt, but that the Sumaicha branch having from compulsion mixed much with Mahommedans, and consequently lost caste, have, to cover their disgrace, invented the improbable story of their having been originally Mahommedans. The Mahommedan Summas of Sinde are doubtless converts from the old Rajpoot stock."—MS. Notes by Captain James Holland, Deputy Quarter-Master General, 1838.

by degrees they acquired the complete sovereignty; having either by force or fraud expelled, or subjected to their authority, the aboriginal inhabitants, consisting of three distinct classes, Wagellas, Katties, and Wagum Chowras. Four or five generations after their settlement, the descendants of the five brothers assumed the name of Jharejah, derived from a leader of the tribe named Jharrah, who set his descendants the example of female infanticide, by putting to death his seven daughters in one day.

Cutch continued tranquil under their sway for many years, until the murder of Humeerjee, the chief of the elder branch of the tribe, by another Jharejah, named Jam Rawul. Khengarjee, the son of Humeerjee, on the death of his father, fled to Ahmedabad to seek the assistance of the viceroy, who had married his sister; and this being readily granted, a force was sent into Cutch to reinstate him, as chief of the tribe, in his rights, which had been usurped by the murderer of his father. On the approach of the viceroy's army, Jam Rawul fled with his adherents to Kattiwar, and founded the town of Nuwanuggur, which is possessed by his descendants at the present day; and Khengarjee assumed the sovereignty of Cutch and Moorvee in Kattiwar, with the title of Rao or Rawul, A. D. 1549.

From the time of Khengarjee until that of Rahiden, A. D. 1666, the succession continued according to the law of primogeniture. Pragjee, the third son of the latter prince, murdered his elder brother, Jewajee, and the second brother,

Nongaljee, having died in the interim, Pragjee, on the death of his father in 1698, ascended the musnud, to the prejudice of his nephews, Kianjee, the son of Jewajee, and Kallajee, the son of Nongaljee. To the former he gave the command of Moorvee in Kattiwar, which his descendants still retain; the latter retired into the Abrassa, and took possession of the principal towns in that district, where his descendants have ever since possessed the chief influence. Pragjee was succeeded, in the year 1716, by his son, Goregee, a brave and enterprizing prince, who had distinguished himself by his courage and conduct during the lifetime of his father, but whose reign is not marked by any occurrence of note: he was succeeded by his son, Rao Daisul.

Rao Daisul ascended the throne, A. D. 1719. At no period was Cutch so respectable as during his rule. He not only repelled four armies despatched from Ahmedabad by the emperor's deputy, to enforce the payment of tribute, but sent his troops across the frontier, and established military posts in Sinde, Parkhur, and Okhamundel, by which steps he checked the predatory horse from the two former quarters, and piracy at the latter. He also took possession of various towns and villages along the southern coast of the Gulf of Cutch, to which he laid claim on account of his relationship to the Rajah of Moorvee; and, notwithstanding all these expensive exertions, exclusive of many improvements he carried on in his own territories, he died at an advanced age, leaving a treasury well stocked with money. The latter ten years of his life were embittered by the unkindness of his son, the Prince Lacca, who threw him into confinement, and also had his celebrated minister, Sett Deokurn, assassinated.

Lacca assumed the supreme authority about the year 1745. The character and forms of the durbar were entirely changed by the luxurious and extravagant splendour that were introduced during his reign, which lasted about ten years after the decease of his father. The advanced posts placed by Rao Daisul in Parkhur and Sinde were driven out; and his son, afterwards Rao Gore, rose in open rebellion against him. Either two or three ministers were put to death during this reign. Poonjah Sett, the son of the celebrated Deokurn Sett, minister of Rao Daisul, was disgraced and dismissed; and the Prince Gore retired to, and resided at, Moondra for the last seven years of his father's life. Forces were frequently sent against him, but were invariably unsuccessful; and although none of the neighbouring powers attempted to invade Cutch in Rao Lacca's time, and his whole strength was therefore disposable, yet it was in vain exerted to subdue the rebellion, headed by his own son, in the very heart of his dominions. He also made an abortive attack on the town and fort of Terah in the Abbrassa, the patrimony of Soomrajee Jharejah, in which he was beaten off, and obliged to return to his capital discomfited.

On the death of Rao Lacca, his only legitimate son, in 1760 Gore, was unanimously acknowledged, although his father had tried to secure the accession for one of his numerous illegitimate children. Poonjah Sett, as soon as he heard of Rao Lacca's death, hastened to Bhooj, in the expectation of being made minister; but he was treated with undisguised contempt and hostility; and hearing that a plot had been formed to assassinate him, he fled to Sinde, and the situation he had aspired to was filled by a distant relative of his own called Jeewun Sett. Cutch was invaded no less than four times by the Sindians during this reign; and on each of these occasions, the country was desolated and plundered, although the invaders did not succeed in forming a permanent settlement. Two of the inroads were headed by Gholam Shah Calora in person, and two of them by his son Meean Surufraz Khan. The former wished to compel the Rao to give him his sister in marriage; but after a treaty had been entered into, in which this stipulation stood as an article, it was evaded, and Gholam Shah was glad, on his second invasion, to content himself with the daughter of the chief of Khauker, whose family stood next in pretensions to the throne.

The inability of Cutch to withstand the power of Sinde was clearly demonstrated by these events; for although the Rao engaged mercenaries from the Nuwab of Rahidenpoor, the Jam of Nuwanuggur, the chief of Moorvee, and others, yet even with all this foreign aid, had it not been for Poonjah Sett, (who first instigated Gholam Shah to the attack, but afterwards repented, a..d persuaded him to return to Hyderabad,) it seems from all accounts probable that the Cutch government would then have been subverted. When the Sindians retired, Poonjah Sett was made minister; but soon after the Rao presented him with his own hand with a bowl of poison, and ordered him to drink it in his presence, merely because he had recommended an adherence to the articles of the treaty. His son Deojee Sett accepted the office of minister about three years subsequent to this, and likewise met an untimely fate by poison.

On quitting Cutch, Gholam Shah left a garrison of 5000 men at Luckput Bunder, which was then a petty town. He also proceeded to build an embankment to prevent the waters of the Indus from falling into the sea through the eastern branch of that river, which passes close to Luckput; and by this unjustifiable act he converted a fertile plain, which yielded from rice cultivation a revenue of eight lacs of cories annually to the Bhooj durbar, into a dreary salt marsh. When Gholam Shah died, his son Surufraz Khan recalled his troops from Luckput, but, as before stated, he twice after this entered Cutch with a considerable force, and devastated a great part of the country before he quitted it.

The garrisons on the part of Cutch in Ballumba, and other places, on the northern coast of Kattiwar, were expelled by the dependants of the Jam about this time; and, instead of resenting these injuries, or at least attempting it, the Rao gave up his whole time and thoughts to the most unheard of cruelty and sensuality. He kept a body of negroes about his person, who allowed no one but the partakers of his disgusting and depraved orgies to approach him. At length the ladies of the durbar prevailed on some of the principal officers to confine the Rao; and whilst he was under this temporary restraint, the whole of the negroes were either put to death, or fled to the adjacent countries. The Rao was so much irritated, that, on being released, he proceeded to Mandavie in disgust, and there occupied himself in building a fine palace, which, however, he never completely finished.

After stating these facts, it is almost superfluous to say, that Rao Gore was a cruel and blood-thirsty tyrant. Exclusively of the revolting instances already detailed, he killed with his own hand his brother Mansingjee, simply because he discovered that he had obtained the favours of a female who had declined his visits; and it is estimated, that in the course of his reign, a period of nineteen years, he sacrificed more than thirty ministers to his rage or rapacity. He left two sons, the prince Rahiden, and Pruthiraj, commonly called Bhyjee Bawa, the former of whom succeeded him.

Rao Rahiden began to reign in 1778, at the early age of fourteen. His mother had appointed a Lohana, by name Dewichund, minister; and it was supposed, from the intercourse they afterwards carried on, that her connexion with him had been criminal, even during Rao Gore's lifetime. The young prince had been accustomed from his infancy to hear of and see scenes of bloodshed and vice; and he quickly afforded proof that he was a most apt scholar in such matters, and needed not the dying exhortations of his father to revenge his mother's infidelity on the tribe (Lohana), to which her paramour belonged. He very soon replaced the negroes who had been turned out or destroyed some years before; and with their assistance he put to death in one day the minister Dewichund, together with his three brothers, and above two hundred of their followers.

A Banian minister was next set up under the auspices of a negro jemidar, named Mecraj; but these ill-assorted authorities soon quarrelled. Parties arranged themselves on each side; and whilst the Rao was indulged in the inner apartments with a few companions in deeds of abandoned lust and profligacy, the palace was daily deluged with the blood of those who were contending for his favour. Some of the most desperate of the negroes were banished, and others put out of the way by poison, which, it is even asserted, the Rao himself mixed with their food, to rid himself of their continual importunities; but those who remained of this class had influence enough to obtain the Rao's order to destroy the Banian, which was done without delay in the public durbar.

On hearing of these proceedings, many of the district officers affected to consider themselves freed from all allegiance to Bhooj. Mandavie, however, and some other important places, continued obedient to the Rao; who, having recently adopted the Mussulman religion, resolved to force his subjects to follow his example, which he determined to do by destroying all the Hindoo temples and images. This mad project he first tried at Mandavie, whether he had gone for the express purpose; but the Brahmins and Banians, who form a large portion of the population, opposed him, and threatened, according to their mode of enforcing their wishes, to commit "traga"* on themselves. The Rao, to let them clearly comprehend how careless he was of such denunciations, drew his sword and wounded five or six of them, before his attendants could seize his hand. He then gave directions that the town should be pillaged; an outrage which was happily prevented, by the rich merchants bribing the garrison to oppose the miscreants who had gladly hastened to carry the Rao's orders into execution. In the meantime, the Rao was himself in great danger from the exasperated feelings of the inhabitants, who attacked him and his escort, and obliged them to make a rapid retreat to Bhooj; where, as a compensation for the disappointment he had met with, and the opposition offered to him at Mandavie, he adopted the plan of moving about the streets habited as a fukeer, and accompanied by a body of his negroes, who put every man whom they met to death, unless he was able and willing to repeat the Mahommedan creed.

It now became notorious that the Rao was de-

* "Traga" consists in sacrificing one of their number, that his blood may rest on the head of their oppressor.

ranged; and after two or three attempts to place him under restraint, in which measure his brother Bhyjee Bawa and the ladies of the palace concurred, he was seized by a body of troops which had been secretly called in from Anjar. In one of the various unsuccessful attempts made to secure his person, which he constantly baffled through the vigilance and ferocity of his negroes, the then minister Kotaree Waga, and above three hundred people, were destroyed in cold blood in one of the palace yards, by the Rao and his desperate associates. From this time the Rao was lodged in confinement; but his brother Bhyjee Bawa being too young to assume the direction of affairs, the government was conducted by twelve commanders of mercenary troops, who appear to have been all Mahommedans, and who were guided by the authority of Dhosul Vain, the principal member of their body.

Among these leaders was Futteh Mahommed, a native of Sinde. This person appears to have been endowed with capacity and courage. Finding the government of Dhosul Vain at once weak and odious, he successfully intrigued with the troops, with the ministers by whom the civil business of the government was still conducted, and with some of the Jharejahs; until, in the year 1792, he was enabled to expel Dhosul Vain and his colleagues, and to transfer the reins of government into his own hands. He conducted the affairs of Cutch with firmness and ability for ten years, until Bhyjee Bawa, in whose name he administered the government, became of age, and began to feel the hardship of his exclusion from the regency. Hunsraj and the other ministers who were dissatisfied with the predominance of Futteh Mahommed, availed themselves of this feeling; and seizing the opportunity of his casual absence from the capital, they carried off Bhyjee to Mandavie, of which Hunsraj was at that time in charge. The wealth and respectable character of Hunsraj, the junction of the other ministers, and the popular manners of Bhyjee, joined to the goodness of his cause, soon drew the majority to his party; while Futteh Mahommed was glad to abandon Bhooj, and to compromise his claim to the administration for the possession of the fort and dependencies of Anjar.

The death of Bhyjee, which happened in 1802, six months after the revolution, restored the ascendancy of Futteh Mahommed. Hunsraj was a merchant, and his wealth and popularity were insufficient to make up for the want of knowledge and confidence in military affairs. He withdrew to Mandavie, leaving Bhooj to be captured by Futteh Mahommed, while Luckput Bunder, Moondra, Bitta, and Seesagud, with their districts, remained in the hands of independent chiefs,* who, although three of them professed Mahommedanism, were all close confederates of Hunsraj. These parties were supported entirely by their mercenary troops, consisting of Arabs, Sindees, and Mussulmans of Cutch. The Jharejahs appear to have possessed but little weight, and to

* Mahommed Meyan Sotah, who enacted so prominent a part afterwards, was one of these, and also Malik Mahommed.

have taken little interest in the struggle; some remained at their forts entirely neutral, others served the contending parties for pay; and although the Rao's person was in the hands of Futteh Mahommed, and Hunsraj had not even the shadow of legitimate authority, the greater part of the Bhyaud were entertained in his service, or attached to his party. Futteh Mahommed proceeded with vigour against such of these as came within his reach; he fomented their family quarrels; he besieged their forts; he levied contributions on various pretences, as well to fill his treasury as to gratify his revenge. His necessities obliged him also to impose numerous and severe taxes and fines on the merchants and ryots; but although these proceedings naturally created general discontent, there seems to have been no attempt to form any combination against him. He continued to govern the capital and the greater part of the Rao's territories, and to carry on depredations on the possessions of his rivals until his death; and the name of the "Jemidar" is now as much respected in Cutch as that of any of the Raos, his predecessors in authority. The death of Futteh Mahommed took place in 1813;—it was preceded by that of Hunsraj, and shortly followed by that of Rao Rahiden.

SECTION II.

FROM THE COMMENCEMENT OF THE BRITISH CONNEXION, TO THE CONCLUSION OF THE TREATY OF 1816.

WE have now arrived at a stage in the History of Cutch when its connexion with the British Government forms the chief part of the detail; and it is here necessary, before proceeding to relate the consequences of the death of Futteh Mahommed, to revert a little, in order to trace the various negotiations which took place. At one of the periods, 1801–2, when Hunsraj, the governor of Mandavie, had gained a temporary ascendancy, he entreated the assistance of the Bombay Government, in the name of Rao Rahiden, for the purpose of allaying the dissensions between himself and Futteh Mahommed, which destroyed the peace of the country; and, to obtain this mediation, he offered to cede Cutch to the Honourable Company, provided the capital was reserved for the residence of the Rao, and arrangements were made for the future support of his Highness. During the next two years, another proposal was received at Bombay to subsidize a body of British troops for the protection of Cutch, which was followed also by a third a short time after (1804), in which both Hunsraj and Futteh Mahommed concurred.

But it was not the policy nor wish of the British government to form any closer alliance with the state of Cutch than what would merely gain for its own subjects, and those of its allies, protection against the unruly dependents of the Rao: and, accordingly, the only agreements entered into with the chieftains above-named, in 1809, were a provision for the suppression of piracy, which had been carried on to a great extent from all the northern ports; and another for the security of Kattiwar and Guzerat, by a stipulation that none of his Highness's troops should cross to the eastward of the Runn or Gulf of Cutch. In return for these engagements, the British government undertook to adjust the settlement of some pecuniary claims made by the Bhooj durbar on the Jam or Prince of Nuwanuggur, but declined to interfere further in the affairs of Cutch than merely to warn the government of Sinde against any attempt at the conquest of that country which the Ameers had shown a disposition to effect.

These arrangements, unfortunately, did not accomplish the object of the English government. The shores of Cutch continued to swarm with pirates, who committed their depredations in the most audacious manner, and to the interruption of all commerce. Sewiraj, the son of Hunsraj;

who had succeeded his father in the command of Mandavie, encouraged these outrages by conniving at the escape of the most daring offenders; and further added to the evil, by imposing a tax on all vessels, not even excepting those furnished with British passes, which entered the Gulf of Cutch. Several of the Company's cruizers were employed in checking these piracies; but they, nevertheless, increased to such an extent, that the Bombay government at length resolved to send an agent to remonstrate with the Mandavie authorities, as well as to obtain payment of a sum of money due to the Honourable Company, and his Highness the Guicawar, by Sewiraj Hunsraj.

The person selected for this purpose was Captain James M'Murdo, a gentleman whose talents and accomplishments fully qualified him for the difficult task. A considerable marine force was placed at his disposal, and he was instructed to collect information respecting the haunts and strength of the pirates;—a duty which he accomplished often at great personal risk, and in a manner highly satisfactory to government. This officer had been but a few days at Mandavie when his penetration enabled him to discover that the pirates not only received protection at that place, but were even permitted to remain unpunished under the immediate eye of Futteh Mahommed. A ship freighted with property to a considerable amount, belonging to Shah Darab, a prince of Cabul, was plundered in the Gulf of Cutch, by a miscreant named Nackwa Hussun, who carried his ill-gotten wealth to Bhooj, where he was allowed to squander it openly in every kind of dissipation.

With Sewiraj Hunsraj, who satisfied all demands, Captain M'Murdo was able to come to an amicable agreement; but matters had scarcely been settled at Mandavie, when his attention was strongly attracted to Futteh Mahommed, who had now also begun to show his disregard of the stipulation of 1809. Bodies of banditti from the province of Wagur were daily permitted to cross into Kattiwar, which they ravaged and laid waste. A Sindee assassin of a British officer, (Captain Phelan,) who had escaped from Nuwanuggur, was employed in the Bhooj durbar; the notorious pirate, Nackwa Hussun, with many others of the same description, were publicly encouraged to reside in that capital; and, as if all these violations of a sacred compact were insufficient, Futteh Mahommed himself proceeded to lead a force across the Runn into Parkur, and established a garrison at Santilpoor, a village on the Gazerat frontier, with the avowed purpose of extending his authority in that quarter.

These various infringements of the treaty were not allowed to pass without a spirited remonstrance upon the part of Captain M'Murdo, who, having concluded his arrangements at Mandavie, had retired to Moorvee in Kattiwar, whence he reminded the Jemidar of his engagements, and urged him to maintain them. He called on him to make restitution of the property of Shah Darab, who had solicited the intercession of the Bombay government, and insisted on the immediate surrender of the Sindee murderer, and the pirate, as the only means of removing a most degrading suspicion from Futteh Mahommed himself. Through this representation the garrison at Santilpore was withdrawn, and negociations were in progress for the punishment of the Wagur plunderers, &c. when Futteh Mahommed died. Having thus supplied the broken link, we now proceed to follow the regular chain of the narration.

On the death of Futteh Mahommed, the government of Cutch devolved quietly on his two eldest sons, Hussain and Ibrahim Meyans. Nothing could be more dissimilar than the characters of these young men. Ibrahim Meyan possessed talent, courage, and energy, with the two last of these qualities in excess; although the younger of the two, he had already taken an active part in the affairs of the state; and he had been entrusted with the command of the important fortress of Kunkote in Wagur, while his brother, who was understood to be of a weak, slow, and vacillating disposition, had been retained at Bhooj under his father's own eye and direction. For some years before his death, Futteh Mahommed had been chiefly guided by the counsels of Jugjeewan Mehtah, a Nagur Brahmin, of fair reputation, in whose integrity he reposed implicit confidence, and to whose advice it was his earnest and dying request that his sons would pay respect and obedience. The influence, however, of this individual had given great dissatisfaction to many of those who were connected by the ties of blood with the Jemidar, and had not only been the cause of much jealousy to his sons, but had proved particularly irksome to their mother, Jumalbhye, a woman of an intriguing disposition, much under the guidance of Mahommed Meyan Sotah, the soi-disant lord of Moondra, one of the most turbulent characters of the period, to whom she was nearly related. The angry feelings of these members of his family on this account had required all Futteh Mahommed's decision to restrain them, and they now broke forth with redoubled violence on his death. On hearing of that event, Ibraham Meyan instantly returned from Kunkote, and, under the pretence of assembling his friends to assist at the ceremonies of his father's funeral, he invited Mahommed Meyan Sotah, Malik Mahommed, Dossul Vain, and other Mahommedan officers, to Bhooj, where a party was immediately formed against Jugjeewan Mehtah, and a plan entered into for putting him to death.

Hussain Meyan, Futteh Mahommed's eldest son, does not appear to have been entrusted to the full extent with the designs of these conspirators; either from an idea that he was partial to the intended victim, or that his timid and irresolute character rendered him unfit, in their estimation, for any measure which required secrecy and decision. The plot, however, was discovered by the vigilance of an Arab Jemidar, named Ahya, who had obtained employment in the service of the durbar, through the patronage of Jugjeewan, and who, on hearing of his danger, came boldly forward, together with his countrymen, and declared their united intention of defending the Mehtah's life and property against all attack.

Matters had reached this crisis, when Rao Rahiden died; and an event occurred, which, from its adding religion to the other causes of dissension, was calculated to inflame the rage of the parties to the uttermost. That unhappy prince, who had long been confined on account of insanity, among his other wild eccentricities, had always affected a fiery zeal for the Mahommedan faith, and had even attempted, when not under personal restraint, to spread it by the sword throughout his dominions. Latterly, his ravings had been entirely on the subject of religion; he had adopted all the austerities of the most devoted enthusiast, and had left directions that his body should be interred in a small mosque, which he had erected for this particular purpose within the precincts of the palace. A request of this nature was too much in accordance with the religious prejudices of Ibrahim Meyan and his Mussulman associates to be received with indifference. They lost not a moment in preparing to give effect to it in the most open and solemn manner; and they had made every arrangement for the funeral, according to the forms prescribed by their creed, when Jugjeewan Mehtah, accompanied by four or five hundred Rajpoots, forcibly seized the corpse, and burned it with great display and ceremony, agreeably to the customs of the Hindoos.

This proceeding had been adopted chiefly at the instigation of the ladies of the palace, who viewed the proposed interment in the light of a profanation. Ibrahim Meyan and his party were either too much taken by surprise, or had really not power sufficient to prevent its completion, and the ashes of Rao Rahiden were deposited with those of his ancestors; but it is almost needless to add, that Jugjeewan Mehta's conduct was esteemed by the Mahommedans as an act of atrocious sacrilege; and while it thus exasperated his enemies to the utmost, and unfortunately excited against him the general feelings of a powerful and military class of the community, it had also the more fatal effect, as will afterwards appear, of diminishing his popularity with the Arabs, his recent defenders. In this state of affairs, intrigues immediately commenced regarding the succession to the throne, and were carried on with the virulence of party spirit for several weeks. Jugjeewan Mehtah and the principal Jharejah chiefs declared in favour of Ladoba, the lawful son of Bhyjee Bawa, and nephew of the late Rao Rahiden; while the opposite faction resolved to elevate Maun Sing, the son of that prince, by a slave girl.

Both these competitors were young, and ignorant of state affairs. Either of the two would have answered the general purposes of the Mahommedan party, who merely wished to place a puppet on the throne, that they might advance their own lawless designs, under the cover of his name and authority; and Ladoba, from being the younger and more legitimate, would in all probability have been preferred, had not the private feelings of

Ibrahim Meyan interfered, and fixed the election on his rival. To explain this circumstance, we must enter briefly into the history of Ibrahim Meyan. About two years before the period at which we have arrived, that young man had formed an attachment for Kesser Bye, the sister of Maun Sing, who, either from affection or ambitious motives, returned his regard, while her brother encouraged his stolen visits at the palace. The intercourse between the lovers was exposed, by a Marwarry Jemidar, named Malum Sing, to Futteh Mahommed, whose conduct on this occasion evinced the superiority of his character. A connexion with the family of the Rao, now easily within his reach, would have added much to his personal respectability, and might have been a sure means of continuing his power to his descendants; but he disdained to purchase such an advantage at the expence of his duty and his reputation, and not only peremptorily forbade his son's further visits at the durbar, but forced him to leave the capital and remain in Wagur. On his return to Bhooj after his father's death, Ibrahim Meyan renewed his intimacy with Kesser Bye, at whose entreaties he engaged to support her brother's pretensions, to the exclusion of the lawful heir. Mahommed Meyan Sotah received a bribe of 50,000 cories; and, by their united influence, Maun Sing was raised to the throne by the name of Rao Bharra, or Bharmuljee.

No opposition appears to have been made to this election by the Jharejahs, many of whom remained in their own possessions, indifferent to the passing events, while the others were either bribed to compliance, or afraid to object. Rao Bharmuljee was eighteen years of age when he ascended the throne. His previous life had been passed in the gloomy monotony of the palace, and his elevation made but little change in his situation. Except on occasions when he was required to appear in public as a pageant, he and his cousin Ladoba were alike kept in strict confinement, where they are said to have lived together in terms of the closest intimacy, and even to have engaged in plans for the subversion of the influence of the Moondra chieftain, who, in the name of Hussain Meyan, soon possessed himself of all the authority, and contrived to fill Bhooj with his mercenary troops. All that two young princes so situated were able to attempt, was not likely to be effectual; but the haughty and overbearing conduct of Mahommed Meyan Sotah at length had the effect of rousing the slumbering energies of Hussain Meyan himself, who, disgusted at the little consideration which had been shown him, privately abandoned the Mussulman party, and made overtures to that headed by Jugjeewan Mehtah.

Meanwhile the British government had, subsequently to the death of Futteh Mahommed, renewed its application to Hussain Meyan, who, after some negociations, requested an agent should be sent to Bhooj. The person selected for this employment was Ragoba Appa, a man of competent talent and experience, with whom I have often conversed, and who was directed to adopt the most conciliatory demeanour in his intercourse with the Cutch Government. On his arrival at Bhooj, he found the parties in the state just detailed, and by his interposition confirmed the renewed friendship between the Methah and Hussain Meyan, both of whom he found favourable to the object of his mission. The consequence of Ragoba Appa's proceedings was an invitation to Captain M'Murdo, who was still at Moorvee, to visit Bhooj, and a remonstrance to Hussain Meyan on the part of Jugjeewan Mehtah, who, as yet supported by the Arabs, and now inspired with confidence by the presence of the British agent, declared his determination not to serve the Durbar in any capacity till Mahommed Meyan Sotah was dismissed. Hussain Meyan summoned up resolution to comply with the Mehtah's request; but Mahommed Meyan Sotah showed no readiness to quit Bhooj, and even attempted, by threats and entreaties, to obtain an order forbidding the approach of Captain M'Murdo. Finding, however, his efforts unsuccessful, he retired to Moondra, in the greatest indignation and disgust. Ibrahim Meyan, though equally hostile to the measures which had been adopted by his brother and Jugjeewan Mehtah, continued to linger at the capital, watching the issue of events, and sunk in a vortex of profligacy and intrigue.

Captain M'Murdo was received by the authorities at Bhooj with respect, and found Jugjeewan Mehtah and Hussain Meyan apparently inclined to be on the most amicable terms with the British Government. On the subject of Santilpore, which became a matter of discussion, they excused themselves, by declaring that they considered the Cutch Durbar had a right to send troops to that place; the spirit of the treaty of 1809 being, as they understood it, to prevent incursions into the territories of the Honourable Company and its allies, among whom they did not include the Nawaub of Rahidenpoore, to whom Santilpore belonged. They acknowledged that Futteh Mahommed had invited the infamous Nackwa Hussun to Bhooj after his plundering Prince Darab's property, but denied the value of the effects seized; there being, as they asserted, nothing more than a few Persian ornaments, which they professed their willingness to restore. The pirate himself, they admitted, was in the service of Mahommed Meyan Sotah, from whom they agreed to demand him, and to deliver him up to the British Government for punishment. They were further ready to give up the Sindee assassin, provided he could be discovered in Cutch; and they also confessed the justice of our demands against Wagur, to chastise the plunderers of which province they offered to send a force, and invited Captain M'Murdo to accompany it. Hussain Meyan freely acknowledged the imbecility of his administration, and expressed his readiness to accept the mediation of the British Government, whose good offices, he said, he had before intended to solicit in assisting to settle the disturbed state of Cutch, and to enable him to place the resources of the country in the hands of legitimate authority.

In conformity with these proposals, which,

though evasive in many respects,, showed some proof of a desire to obtain the favour of the English Government, the Durbar applied to the Moondra chief for the surrender of the pirate Hussun, and Hussain Meyan marched 12th April, with 3000 men into Wagur, whither he was accompanied by Captain M'Murdo. Mahommed Meyan Sotah's laconic and cavalier reply to the application just alluded to, will demonstrate the temper of that chief, as well as his regard for truth—the pirate having been actually seen in his employment at the very time his letter was written—and his respect for the Government of Cutch. It was in these terms: "You mention the English M'Murdo is arrived, let me know what he communicates. The Nackwa Hussun is at Curachee." On the advance of the above force into Wagur, many of the chieftains repaired to Hussain Meyan's camp, and submitted to his authority. He established garrisons at Palanswa, Rhapoor, &c. and the province ostensibly returned to a state of order; but, as his means were too limited to secure an effectual and permanent tranquillity, he shortly after returned to Bhooj, and Captain M'Murdo proceeded to Kattiwar, perfectly satisfied of the inability of the reigning powers in Cutch to restrain their troublesome dependents.

During this interval, Ibrahim Meyan, although he had accompanied the Wagur expedition, had continued a member of the Moondra party, and had never ceased to upbraid and condemn his brother for his adherence, to what he termed, the British interests. On the return of the latter to the capital, Ibrahim established himself at Kunkote, and encouraged the Belah, and other plunderers of Wagur, by every means in his power; finally, he declared open war against his brother and the Bhooj authorities, and, together with Ascaran Sa, a troublesome and turbulent character, with whom he had allied himself and Mahommed Meyan Sotah, committed extensive depredations in the district of Anjar, and forcibly took possession of the town and fort of Futteh Ghud. While the eastern side of Cutch was thus a prey to rapine and disorder, Mandavie was also the scene of contention and bloodshed. Dhosul Vain and Malik Mahommed, at the instigation of the Moondra chieftain, made an attempt to wrest it from Sewiraj Hunsraj, their employer, but were detected and defeated. Civil war raged with all its fury; nor had the durbar any means to check or suspend its horrors. Three or four distinct factions divided the country, all of whom joined only in one object, the plunder of the labouring and peaceable classes, who were reduced to beggary and starvation by their manifold extortions. The Wagur banditti, seizing the opportunity, extended their ravages both at home and abroad. Sixty villages belonging to the Guicowar and Peishwa in Kattiwar, had now been destroyed; and as no effectual means were taken to prevent these outrages, the British government at length intimated that their troops, and those of their allies, would no longer be restrained from following the marauders to their own haunts at Wagur; that the Bhooj durbar would be liable to the charges of the equipment of the force to be so employed; and that certain instalments, due to his Highness, the Rao, by the Jam of Nawanuggur, would be applied to the indemnification of the losses already sustained. This intimation, on the part of the English government, added to the successes of the Moondra party, which Hussain Meyan had no power to combat, produced a powerful effect on the weak and timid character of that chief. After some vacillation, he at length determined to throw himself on the mercy of his brother, to whom, through the influence of their mother, he was reconciled; and Cutch became once more at the disposal of men inimical to British influence; as proofs of which, the promise formerly made, that the pirate Hussun, who was now a prisoner at Bhooj, should be delivered up, was disregarded,—the Sinde murderer was openly retained in the service of Ibrahim Meyan,—and he and his party adopted every means in their power to show their indifference respecting the claims which had been preferred.

The re-union of the brothers was a prelude to a cruel and barbarous tragedy. Jugjeewan Mehtah's habits of business rendered him at first necessary to them as a minister; but his offences against the party now in power had been too grievous to be forgiven; and the former resolution of assassinating him was soon renewed. His popularity with the Arabs had been for some time gradually on the decline. Most of them, in fact, had incurred large private debts to him, besides receiving considerable advances of pay from him as a public servant of the durbar, and they now viewed him only in the light of a creditor, from whose importunities they were anxious to be relieved. Under these circumstances, a confidential agent from Ibrahim Meyan found no great difficulty in corrupting the popular Jemidar Ahya; and the whole Arab body finally consented to withdraw their protection from Jugjeewan, in consideration of an acquittance of all sums of money which had been advanced to them from the public treasury, and a present of 6000 cories to each of their leading officers. These proceedings were carried on with the most profound secrecy; and it is but charity to suppose that Hussain Meyan was not made acquainted with them until too late to prevent their fatal effects. The ill-fated object of the conspiracy did not entertain the slightest suspicion of his danger, till the designs of his enemies were ripe for execution, and he saw his residence suddenly surrounded and attacked by a body of armed men, under the command of Ibrahim Meyan in person, and Jaffeer Sotah, the brother of the Moondra chief. The presence of two such leaders, whom Jugjeewan had always known to be the most inveterate of his foes, could leave not a moment's doubt on his mind as to the intentions of the assailants. In despair, therefore, he prepared to make the most determined resistance, and, supported by his domestics, actually continued to baffle all attempts to effect an entrance into his house for six hours. At the end of that period, three pieces of ordnance having been brought to bear on the door, further defence was hopeless; and he was inveigled into a capitulation by a promise sacredly given, that he might proceed to the palace of Futteh Mahommed's sons to plead for his life. The assault had been so protracted, that Ibrahim Meyan had retired before this understanding was entered into; but a negro Jemidar of some importance in his service, named Ibrahim Seedee, who was present, and in whose honour Jugjeewan believed he could repose confidence, having volunteered to become security for the maintenance of the pledge, and even to escort him in safety to the presence of Hussain Meyan, the unfortunate Mehtah went out into the street without hesitation, and accepted his protection. He was then conducted amidst great tumult and confusion, to the gate of Hussain Meyan's residence, where he was appealing to the populace, and imploring his persecutors to spare his life, when Ibrahim Meyan appeared at a window, and, scornfully taunting him with having tried to sell his country to the British, exultingly ordered him to be dispatched; a command which was instantly executed by Jaffeer Sotah and his attendants.

Early in the morning of the same day, Ramchunder Mehtah, the brother of Jugjeewan, on going to pay his usual respects at the durbar, had been entrapped and strangled by order of Ibrahim Meyan, who alleged that he had committed suicide. Another brother, the sole remaining member of the family, named Kooberjee, who had long been in declining health, and who was probably spared by the assassins on account of his utter helplessness and insignificance, having witnessed the ruin of his house, determined not to survive it, and a few days after, caused himself to be buried alive, agreeably to a custom adopted by Brahmins, of invoking the vengeance of the Almighty upon those who have oppressed them. The bloody work of the conspirators being completed, the Mehtah's house was given over to the pillage of the soldiery, and the most valuable part of his property was confiscated to the state, or rather to the private use of Hussain and Ibrahim Meyans, who took the administration of affairs into their own hands, assisted by Mehtahs Wullubjee, and Luckmadass. Jugjeewan Mehtah had been much respected at Bhooj, and his murder, under such cruel and afflicting circumstances, excited great disgust among the inhabitants. Hussain Meyan had taken no active or open part in it; and the odium appears chiefly to have fallen on Mahommed Meyan Sotah, and his brother Jaffeer, who retired to Moondra, in order to escape the popular indignation, as well as from a fear that the British government would interfere.

The ferment occasioned by these tragical events had scarcely subsided, when Ibrahim Meyan was as suddenly called to the tribunal of Heaven to answer for his offences. He had, in concert with his brother, Luckmadass, and other associates, appointed a public day, in order to bestow rewards and distinctions on his officers, and particularly on those who had assisted him in the murder of Jugjeewan Mehtah; and the whole assembled in great state at Hussain Meyan's residence for the purpose. Amongst those who presented themselves, in the hope of obtaining notice, was Malum Sing, the Marwarry Jemidar, formerly mentioned as having betrayed Ibrahim Meyan's intrigue with Kesser Bye to Futteh Mahommed, and who now urged a claim of many years' service to the durbar for preferment. Ibrahim Meyan, whose feelings towards the man may be readily conceived, repulsed him with scorn, and the grossest abuse; which the Marwarry immediately resented, by stabbing him mortally on the spot. The scene that followed may be imagined. Hussain Meyan horror-struck, and expecting to be the next victim, rushed with Luckmadass into another apartment; but their apprehension was soon proved to be groundless, for the assassin was instantly cut to pieces, and it was never discovered that he had any confederates.

It is generally understood that Malum Sing went to the levee expressly for the purpose of committing the murder; and this opinion is supported by the fact of his having carried the weapon with which he perpetrated it carefully concealed under his clothes into the assembly. He had just before been relieved from duty at the palace, and he was supposed by many to have been instigated by the Rao; but Bharmuljee, who was then only about eighteen years of age, had previously shown no evil disposition; nor does there seem any good reason for adding this additional sin to his load of crimes. Persons who were well acquainted with the characters of the parties, and who were eye-witnesses of the transaction, do not attribute it to the provocation that was given at the moment; and Ibrahim Meyan's death may probably be referred to his having engaged in an intrigue with a female connected with the Marwarry Jemidar, whose revenge was no doubt sharpened by the insults that were offered to him. Ibrahim Meyan had not attained the age of twenty-five years when he was assassinated. From his depraved habits, and total want of principle, it is scarcely to be supposed that his death would be regretted; but as he was a young man of great liberality, personal bravery, and address, and the only one of his family who inherited any portion of the talent of his father, the old friends of Futteh Mahommed bewailed his loss, as that of the representative, however unworthy, of their Jemidar, and foresaw the immediate ruin of his house, whose power he himself, from a knowledge of the characters of his children, had prophesied would not long survive him.

The murder of his brother excited the greatest consternation in Hussain Meyan's mind. Unable to distinguish between friends and enemies, he resigned himself almost to despair, and, with the timidity natural to his disposition, remained shut up in his house, guarded by the Arabs. His suspicions at first fell upon the Rao, whose palace he ordered to be attacked; and although his Highness solemnly protested his innocence, a body of Arabs was permanently stationed in the durbar; while, in order to guard against future conspiracies, the Marwarry soldiery in Bhooj, amounting to two or three hundred men, were either massacred, or expelled from Cutch. All these events created a great sensation throughout the country. The gates of the capital were kept closed for many days, and scarcely any communication took place among the inhabitants. Hussain Meyan's fears rendered him perfectly incapable of acting with calmness or propriety; and the government being without any efficient head, the Arab Jemidars usurped the whole authority, and for a short time conducted the affairs of the state, levying for their own use heavy fines and contributions. Butchow, Chowbaree, and Rhapoor, with several other towns, taking advantage of the imbecility of the government, declared their independence of Bhooj, and even applied for the support and protection of the British. After a time Hussain Meyan, who had never dared to appear in public since the assassination of his brother, sent to implore the assistance of Mahommed Meyan Sotah; who, well aware, however, of his unpopularity, declined visiting Bhooj on the plea of sickness, but added to the troubles of the country, by directing his retainers to plunder in every direction. During this state of affairs, the Wagur freebooters continued their depredations, and the British government again reminded Hussain Meyan of their claims. His personal apprehensions, and the weakness of his administration, made him now readily grasp at any chance of support; and he willingly offered to send an agent to adjust all differences.

But the incapacity of Hussain Meyan for

government, and the despicable nature of his character, had of late become but too apparent. The troubles he had inflicted on the country were now so grievously felt, that the respectable part of the community determined to be relieved from a chief at once odious and contemptible; and the tide of popular opinion turned entirely in favour of Rao Bharmuljee, who had secretly been carrying on negociations with Sewiraj Hunsraj and the principal Jharejahs. Deputies soon arrived from Mandavie, expressing the readiness of the authorities there to acknowledge the Rao; and Sewiraj himself, with Ascaran Sa and many of the chiefs, assembled troops in support of his cause. Hussain Meyan, whom his Arab Jemidars had in vain attempted to inspire with courage, readily yielded to the current; and when it became evident that his cause was unsupported, he made a virtue of necessity, by entering into a compromise with Bharmuljee, who, on his consenting to leave Bhooj, gave him a grant of Anjar, Butchow, Badurghud, and Kunkote. He was then dismissed with an honorary dress, and proceeded to Anjar, whither he was accompanied by all the Arab mercenaries, none of whom the new government would permit to remain at Bhooj. By these measures all opposition being terminated, the keys of the city were delivered, with every formality, to Rao Bharmuljee, who appointed Sewiraj Hunsraj and Ascaran Sa his ministers; and the country, for the present, was restored to quietness.

The British government had awaited the issue

of events at Bhooj, in the hope that a restoration of legitimate authority would lead to an adjustment of their demands. They now renewed their application to the Rao, and expressed their willingness to receive envoys from his Highness; but the measures of this prince soon showed how averse he was to the establishment of a good understanding. The Cutch durbar had not hitherto been absolutely identified with the plunderers of Wagur; but Bharmuljee settled the question, by openly complimenting Sirmanya, the most notorious of these, with a dress of honour; and he also adopted the violent step of compelling the agent of Captain M'Murdo to quit Bhooj, under the evasive pretence that he would employ Soonderjee Seojee, a horse-contractor for the Honourable Company at Mandavie, as the mediator with the British government.

The tranquillity of Cutch was of short duration. The hereditary chieftain of Kunkote suddenly surprised that town, and expelled Hussain Meyan's garrison; Sewiraj Hunsraj and Ascaran Sa quarrelled before six weeks had elapsed, and the latter left Bhooj to join Mahommed Meyan Sotah, who had raised the standard of rebellion at Moondra, and was collecting troops from every quarter. The country was once more involved in faction and confusion. The Rao assembled a force, and moved against Moondra, which he invested, at the sametime compelling the authorities there to listen to terms. Mahommed Meyan Sotah engaged to surrender his town at the end of one month, provided his Highness would inmediately withdraw his army, and, in proof of his sincerity, he delivered up his brother, Jaffeer Meyan, as a hostage; but before the stipulated period had elapsed, Jaffeer Meyan contrived to escape to Moondra, and assisted his brother in retaining that place in defiance of the durbar.

The government of Rao Bharmuljee soon became exceedingly unpopular. His marriage, which took place on his return from Moondra, attracted crowds to Bhooj, who were treated by him and his public servants with great indignity. He evinced a strong and unaccountable aversion to the Jharejah chiefs, many of whom had been instrumental in restoring him to the throne; and an unwarrantable attack he made on the chief of Assumbia, whose town he destroyed, and on whose family he imposed a large fine, gave great disgust to the whole of these noblemen. Unpopular as the Rao was in his own dominions, his ministers determined to raise him enemies from abroad. A British and Guicowar force had been ordered to reduce Jooriah in Kattiwar, and Sewiraj Hunsraj openly supplied the rebellious authorities of that place with assistance and ammunition.

The easy and unexpected reduction of Jooriah embarrassed the Cutch government much, and opened the Rao's eyes to the danger of his proceedings. He consequently determined, if possible, to make his peace, even thus late, with the British, and to atone for his offences. With this view, he announced his intention of punishing the Wagur banditti, and marched into that district with a formidable army. He reduced Planswa, Rhapoor, and Kanmeer, and likewise put to death the notorious plunderer Sirmanya, whom he had before encouraged and rewarded; but it soon became evident that these measures had their origin in fear not inclination, for he did not remain absent from Bhooj longer than fifteen days, and no effectual steps were taken to prevent the future incursions of the freebooters. It would almost appear that Sirmanya had been killed by chance, or contrary to the Rao's wishes, as he dismissed his family, equally atrocious as himself, with promises of protection.

Rao Bharmuljee's presence in Wagur suspended for a short time the operations of the banditti; but he had scarcely withdrawn his force, when their depredations were renewed with redoubled vigour. Captain M'Murdo's own camp was attacked by them in the neighbourhood of Moorvee. In the space of a few months, one hundred and thirty-six villages in Kattiwar had been plundered, forty thousand head of cattle had been carried off, and property to the amount of eight lacs of rupees damaged and destroyed. In addition to all this, an expense had been incurred by the British and Guicowar governments of above ten lacs of rupees in equipping troops to check these unwarrantable proceedings. Forbearance had been misconstrued by the Bhooj durbar into inability; and as it was now certain that the Rao either wanted the power or the inclination to control his unruly subjects, Captain M'Murdo was instructed to make a specific demand of compensation for the past, and a guarantee against future incursions, together with the surrender of Sirmanya's family, and satisfaction for the insults offered to the British government in having so long delayed, under frivolous pretences, to send an envoy to settle all disputes, as well as for the offensive manner in which the native agent had been forced to leave Bhooj. To these points an explicit answer was required within a given period; and in order clearly to evince the intentions of the allied governments, an army composed of British and Guicowar troops, under the command of Colonel William East, C. B. and Wittul Row Dewanjee, was ordered to advance to the border of the Runn.

Rao Bharmuljee permitted the specified period to elapse without sending any answer to these demands, although, a few days after, he addressed a letter to Captain M'Murdo, couched in general terms, and without any allusion to the articles in question. In consequence of this evasion, the combined troops crossed the Runn at Vensair, and advanced to Wandiah, the chief of which, and many others, immediately threw themselves on the mercy of the allied governments. Proposals had previously been made by the Mandavie and Moondra authorities, both of which had now thrown off their subjection to Bharmuljee, and with them Captain M'Murdo lost no time in entering into a communication, in order to prevent a re-union with the Durbar. He addressed a letter to the Rao, expressing an eager desire that matters might be amicably settled, and still begging agents to be sent for the purpose. To the principal Jharejahs he issued proclamations calculated to inspire them with confidence, and explanatory of the intention of the British Government, which, he assured them, was resolved neither to interfere with their domestic concerns, nor to disturb their repose, so long as they remained quiet in their own domains, but merely, and amicably if possible, to obtain from the Cutch Durbar satisfaction for the indignities which had been received, indemnification for past losses, and security against future depredation. The most prudent measures were taken to prevent any interference with the inhabitants and villages on the line of march; and, by the time the force reached Butchow, the people had recovered their confidence, and supplies were readily afforded.

Meanwhile Rao Bharmuljee had taken no effectual means, either by assembling a force, or by negociation, to prevent the advance of the British army. He had hoped that some assistance would be afforded him by the Ameers of Sinde; but the Bombay government had taken the precaution of previously explaining its intentions to their Highnesses, and had expostulated with them against any interference with the affairs of Cutch. As the crisis approached, he made an attempt to enter into an alliance with Sewiraj Hunsraj, Mahommed Meyan Sotah, and some other chiefs who had combined against him, but without success. He also directed the Jharejahs to assemble at Bhooj, but a few only obeyed the summons, and these apparently with no warlike intentions.

Colonel East's force advanced to Bheemasir, within three marches of the capital and one of Anjar, without any show of opposition. The intention of Captain M'Murdo had been to proceed directly to Bhooj, and there to enter into such a treaty as would meet the wishes of his government; but this arrangement was entirely changed from the detection of one of the most treacherous and cowardly acts that ever was recorded. On the arrival of the army at Bheemasir, it was discovered that a large quantity of wheat, and it is said arsenic, had been thrown into the tank on which the troops chiefly depended for water; and information was at the same time received that all the wells in the direction of Bhooj were poisoned in a similar manner. Although suspicions at first attached to Rao Bharmuljee, it was soon ascertained that the perpetrators of this atrocity were horsemen from Anjar, and that the more immediate agent was Hussain Meyan. Under these circumstances, it became clear that the army ought not to proceed without due caution; and it was necessary, as a temporary measure, to take possession of some post that would secure a constant communication with the friendly shores of Kattiwar. Hussain Meyan was accordingly called on to permit the occupation of Anjar, and its tributary fort of Toona, on the sea side, by a British garrison; but as he objected to this proposal, the force advanced, and a battery was erected against Anjar, which did not surrender until a breach had been rendered practicable. Hussain Meyan was allowed to remain unpunished, and has since lived in obscurity at Moorvee, chiefly on the charity of the Bhooj durbar.

On the reduction of Anjar, which was immediately followed by that of Toona, Captain M'Murdo again addressed the Rao, explaining the cause and necessity of the measures which had been adopted, assuring him that the forts would only be held in trust till an accommodation should be concluded, and again urging him to send agents for the settlement of all disputes. On the day after the surrender of the towns, Mahommed Meyan Sotah made his submission in person at the British camp, and letters were received from the Rao, and Sewiraj Munsraj, of a conciliatory nature.

Under the impression that Bharmuljee's occupation of the throne was considered an usurpation by the chiefs and inhabitants, as well, perhaps, as from some regard to the rights of legitimacy, Captain M'Murdo had been instructed to ascertain the feelings of the Jharejahs towards Ladoba, and if these were favourable, to enter into a treaty with that prince, as the lawful Rao of Cutch. No disposition unfavourable to Bharmuljee was however evinced in any quarter, and it consequently only remained to commence the necessary negociations with him.

It was only on the arrival of the British army at Lackoond, within a few miles of the capital, that agents arrived from Bhooj, expressing the willingness of their master to agree to the proposed terms. The Rao then delivered a bond, with the security of the principal Jharejahs for twenty lacs of rupees, in payment of all demands, besides a promise of two lacs of cories as a yearly tribute; and, after several negociations, a treaty of amity and alliance was concluded between the governments, of which the principal articles, independently of the compensation for past, and security against future depredations, on the part of the durbar, were an engagement on our part to reduce Wagur, &c. to the subjection of the Rao, and the cession of the city and district of Anjar to the British government, in virtue of which, Captain M'Murdo remained at that place as collector and political resident in Cutch.

SECTION III.

FROM THE CONCLUSION OF THE TREATY OF 1816, TO THE CONCLUSION OF THE TREATY OF 1819.

THE terms of the new treaty were highly advantageous to the Rao Bharmuljee. His title to the throne, however dubious, was now acknowledged by the only power in India which could give it stability; Wagur was reduced under subjection by the British troops in the course of a few weeks: and a yearly assessment, in his name, as lord paramount, was laid on its chiefs, at the rate of forty cories for every plough. The refractory authorities of Mandavie, Moondra, Seesaghud, Butchao, &c. seeing the aspect of affairs, at once submitted; and Bharmuljee found his country, for the first time, free from open faction, and himself in undisputed sovereignty.

Of the twenty lacs of rupees, claimed in name of indemnification and expenses, the British government shortly afterwards remitted their own portion, amounting to above eight hundred thousand, together with the yearly tribute of two lacs of cories; a liberality which at first equally surprised and delighted the Rao, who found no great difficulty in raising the remaining balance by fines on his refractory chieftains, and demands, under the title of voluntary contributions, from those who had long enjoyed the revenues of the country. Mahommed Meyan Sotah was the only one of these who declared his inability to afford pecuniary assistance; but the Bhooj government eventually found means to obtain from him nearly six lacs of cories.

Tranquillity being thus restored in Cutch, the British troops, with the exception of a small garrison stationed at Anjar, evacuated the country; and the durbar was left free to adopt its own measures. Luckmadass Wullubjee, already spoken of as the confederate of Hussain Meyan, became minister, with the assistance of Nuthoo Mehtah; and the military advisers of the Rao were Jharejahs Nonghuljee of Vinjan, and Pragjee of Kotree. None of these men were favourably inclined to the British interests, nor could much confidence be reposed in them. Luckmadass, a proud and narrow-minded Brahmin, though a man of talent, had been accused as an accessary in the murder of Jugjeewan Mehtah, and Jharejah Pragjee was known to be faithless and treacherous. Luckily for Bharmuljee, however, he found an able and sincere adviser in his sister Kesser Bhye, a young lady who possessed considerable ability, and who, for a time, was able to guide his conduct, by the maxims of prudence and moderation.

The British interference in Cutch had given great offence, and occasioned much apprehension to the Ameers of Sinde, whose jealousy and fears were not allayed by the repeated explanations they had received from Bombay. They immediately despatched messengers to Bhooj, ostensibly to negociate the payment of a sum of money due at Hyderabad, by a merchant of Luckput, but, in reality, to intrigue with the Rao; and represented the circumstance of our having sent a force into Cutch, in the most exaggerated light to their sovereign lord Mahmood Shah, the king of Cabul, whom they entreated to remonstrate with the supreme government of India. Intelligence was soon after received at Bombay of preparations for the assemblage of a force at Shikarpoor; and various rumours were afloat of the march of the Afghaun army towards Sinde. But the Sindian ambassadors, on their arrival at Bhooj, soon divulged their real object. They represented to the durbar the danger of forming a connexion with neighbours so powerful as the British; and they even went so far as to insinuate that, in case of necessity, the army of the Ameers was at the disposal of Rao Bharmuljee. No means were left untried to break up the alliance; but the Cutch government, fortunately for itself, and whatever may have been its real feelings, was proof against their solicitations; and the vakeels returned to Hyderadad without having gained any apparent object.

The mission from Sinde, however, to the Bhooj durbar was soon followed by a remonstrance from the king of Cabul himself to the governor-general of India; in which, after expressing his conviction, that the invasion of the Rao's territories was unsanctioned by his lordship, his Majesty proceeds to claim for himself the sovereignty of Cutch, and to require the renunciation of all interference with that country as a component portion of the Afghaun dominions. A letter from the vizier Futteh Khan Barukzye, which accompanied the king's communication, was still more explicit. It stated, that "news at this time has been brought to the royal feet, that some Feringees of the English tribe, having more boldness than discretion, have shown a disposition to create disturbance, and have extended the hand of encroachmont to the country of Cutch, which is the frontier district of the royal dominions. On hearing of this, the mind of his majesty was disturbed with anger, and his royal mandate was issued, that letters should be dispatched to all the Nazims of the provinces of the kingdom, enjoining them to be prepared, and to expect the receipt of further orders." The vizier proceeds to say, that, "if the people in question should not be restrained, and if intelligence of a similar occurrence should again reach the king, that two lacs of Douranies and Elats, four dustahs of Emacks and Tymoorias, Huzarahs as numerous as ants and grasshoppers, the tribes of Ghiljes, and Andarees, and Tonkas, and Makoos, and Khookhanies, and Kohistanies; the armies composed of the Khusselbashees, and Moghuls, and Kanwaries, and Toorkalans, and Shurnwaries Husmud Khatick, and the Bungoes great and small, and the Daoodyes, and the Rohaus, and the Mahmoodzyes, and the Yoozafzyes both of the hills and of the plains, and the men of Nagaon and Aman, and the Nuwab Suboolund Khan, ruler of Kutch Walliah, and the governor of the Derahs, and of Mooltan, and the army of Beloches, Burohooe, and Muzara, and Rokunood Dowlah, and Ameerood Dowlah, with the Beloche army, and a train of artillery, and a Shaha Khaneh,—all these forces, numerous as the waves of the sea, having collected agreeably to the royal orders, will surround these people, and annihilate them, and friendship will be at an end. It is best, therefore, that you should prohibit them, and restrain them from these improper proceedings."

This high-sounding epistle, together with the formidable muster-roll of his Majesty's forces, was not likely to excite much alarm in the mind of the Marquis of Hastings, who considered it, or, at all events, determined to treat the whole as forgery. His Lordship addressed a friendly reply to the vizier, in which he declared his conviction that the communications from Cabul were the fabrication of persons ill-disposed to both states, who sought to embroil them with a view to obtain some benefit to themselves; reminded him that Cutch had never at any time formed part of the dominions of the Afghaun monarchy; and shortly explained the object of the British interference; adding, that he necessarily believed the letter fictitious, since he was too well apprized of the knowledge, experience, and sagacity of Futteh Khan, to imagine that he could conceive the British Government would for a moment be influenced by any display of force, and that his information was too enlarged not to know, that though it does not misuse its strength by wantonly trespassing on its neighbours, it has never been attacked without destroying those who unjustly assailed it.

The state of affairs in Cabul was, however, somewhat changed before his lordship's reply reached that kingdom, and the messenger who conveyed it, after having been detained several weeks as a prisoner, by a detachment of Runjeet Sing's army, overtook the vizier at Peshavur ready to take the field against the Sikhs, who were threatening the frontier at Attock. Futted Khan, with that adroitness which native diplomatists generally display, immediately resolved to turn the letter to account, and with the view of impressing his enemies with sentiments favourable to his own interests, ordered a salute to be fired on its reception; at the same time proclaiming aloud through his camp that despatches had been received from the friend of the Cabul government, the Governor-General of India.

To the Marquis of Hastings the vizier replied in the most hyperbolical terms of oriental metaphor; assuring Captain M'Murdo, who had been the medium of communication, that "the sweet and delicious perfume of his lordship's rose-scented letter had ascended, with the most exquisite sensations, to the innermost recesses of his brain;" and that, from the moment he had perused it, he felt the excess of his regard for the British government, between which, and the state of Cabul, he trusted that the "carpet of friendship would ever be spread in the palace of affection." He desired the courier to inform the British agent, that, in the prosecution of his operations against the Sikhs, he not only did not expect an enemy in the English, but looked for their support; that in due time he meant to bring Sinde to its former state of dependence on Cabul; and that, if they had really any views towards that country, he would readily enter into them, and afford his assistance. To complete the farce, he gravely professed ignorance of the letters which had been received at Calcutta, and declared, that he could only account for them by supposing, that a Sindian agent had procured by bribery, impressions of his own and other official seals, from a faithless secretary who had been left at the capital of Cabul.

The Cutch government had, in the meantime, betrayed its utter unworthiness of the confidence and liberality of the British. Strange as it may seem, even the releasing it from a bond of so many lacs of rupees, excited the suspicion of its members; and the effects of the Sindian intrigues were soon visible. The increased power of the Rao only served to swell his arrogance and pride. During an occasional absence of the resident, the durbar determined to seize on the port of Toona; and for this purpose, the Arab mercenaries were recruited at Bhooj, in express opposition to the articles of the late treaty. But these treacherous designs were crushed in their birth by the vigilance and decision of Captain M'Murdo, who called in the assistance of some troops from Okamundel, on the Kattiwar side of the gulf, and insisted on the immediate reduction of the newly raised levies. His demands, after a great deal of evasion, were tardily complied with; and, indeed, much indifference was shown to every proposal emanating from the British government. The Khosas, a predatory tribe inhabiting the desert to the north of Cutch, had at this period commenced their marauding incursions; but nothing could induce the Rao to defend his own territories from these freebooters, much less to enter into any arrangement for the protection of those of his allies.

Evil and ungrateful as was this disposition on the part of the durbar, matters gradually became much worse. Luckmadass and his party, though indifferent, had never wished to come to an absolute rupture with the British government; but their influence speedily declined, and the Rao found far worse counsellors. He became addicted to constant intoxication and the lowest sensuality, and selected, as the associates of his pleasures, men of the meanest and most depraved characters, whose interest and object it appears to have been to instil into his mind constant suspicions of his new allies, and of their representative, Captain M'Murdo. Among these, as particularly worthy of execration, we may here mention Mohunjee Tuckkur, a wretch, who may with justice be called the evil genius of Rao Bharmuljee, and to whom all the subsequent misfortunes of that unhappy prince are mainly to be attributed.

The consequence of all this was soon apparent. The whole power fell into the hands of the Rao's profligate favourites; and every act of tyranny and injustice that could feed his avarice, or minister to his guilty enjoyments, was daily sanctioned. The very influence of the British government, by which it was insinuated, and generally believed, he would be supported under all circumstances, enabled him to obtain enormous sums, as loans, from the merchants and other persons of property; and when this resource failed, every species of extortion was practised. The revenues for eight months in advance were seized from the cultivators of the soil, and twenty lacs of cories were exacted in fines from the household officers and managers of the districts, to be dissipated in the grossest debauchery. Bharmuljee himself was almost never seen outside his apartments; he paid no attention whatever to business, and daily became more odious to his people. He debauched the daughter of Futteh Mahommed, in revenge, as he declared, for Ibrahim Meyan's similar conduct to his sister; and women of all classes were publicly seized in the streets, to be dragged to the palace, and there despoiled of their ornaments and their virtue. No man possessed of any wealth was safe in the country. The Jharejahs, with scarcely an exception, retired to their own estates, and never visited Bhooj; and the ministers themselves, formerly so averse to British influence, having now lost both their property and power entreated the interposition of Captain M'Murdo, as the only means of saving their lives. That officer was not by his instructions authorized to interfere; but, through his influence, he was enabled to obtain the appointment, as a member of the administration, of Ruttunsi Jetta, the nephew of Soondurjee Seojee, long a faithful and meritorious servant of the East India Company, in the hope that his talents and conciliatory manners might gain him such an ascendancy over Bharmuljee, as gradually to withdraw him from his evil habits and associates.

The resident's own efforts were directed to the same object, but unhappily proved fruitless; nor did Ruttunsi unfortunately ever obtain sufficient influence to secure so desirable an end. The Rao's depraved habits and their disastrous effects became daily more aggravating, and at length ended in a crime which showed that all principle and humanity had been discarded and forgotten. Ladoba, the unfortunate son of Bhyjee Bawa, since the elevation of his cousin to the throne, had remained as a kind of state prisoner in the durbar; where, however, he was not rigidly guarded, but even frequently admitted as a companion at the debauched orgies of the Rao. His Highness and he had passed an evening together in drinking, and parted at a late hour with mutual professions of friendship; yet five minutes had scarcely elapsed before Ladoba was attacked by some armed men, in passing through one of the courts of the Palace, and brutally assassinated.

The Rao attempted for a time to deny his participation in this cruel and treacherous transaction, which he declared to have been an unauthorized act of his guards, and even dissembled so far as to seize a musket and threaten to shoot the principal assassin; but it was soon discovered that the murder had been committed by his express orders, issued at the moment Ladoba left him, and that he had himself witnessed it from a window. No punishment was inflicted on the perpetrators of the atrocity; and the chief of these, an Arab Jamidar, named Abdool Kareem, was not only not removed from his situation, but was promoted in rank, and received many additional marks of his master's favour. Three months had not elapsed, however, before the hand of justice overtook this miscreant; for, a cow having been killed in the streets of Bhooj, by a soldier under his command, whom he attempted to shield from the punishment due to such an outrage on the prejudices of the Hindoos, he was put to death, together with the offender, by order of the Rao.

The murder of Ladoba was an act of wanton and uncalled-for tyranny. No provocation had been given on his part, nor could his claims to the throne, now laid aside and forgotten, interfere with the Rao's possession of it, sanctioned as it was by the solemn decision of the Jharejah brotherhood, and the countenance of the British government. We might in charity be inclined to attribute the assassination to frenzy proceeding from intoxication, did it not appear from Bharmuljee's subsequent conduct that his mind was the prey of every suspicion, however unjust or ridiculous, and that his cruelty to Ladoba's family did not cease even with the murder of his unfortunate relative.

This barbarous proceeding on the part of the Rao occasioned much disgust in Cutch. Many of the Jharejah chiefs began now, when too late, to regret their indifference to the better-founded claims of Ladoba to the throne; most of them loudly expressed their abhorrence of his murder; and a feud broke out between the chieftains of Vinjan and Sandan in the Abbrassa, which may be traced to that cause. Bharmuljee's hatred against the Bhyauds had not been diminished by recent events, and he readily seized the opportunity of taking a part in the quarrel, and of levying a heavy fine on Sandan; an act of oppression, which, as will afterwards appear, was a main reason of his losing his throne.

The intelligence of these events reached Bombay, together with an affecting appeal from the father of the widow of the murdered prince, a petty chief in Kattiwar, who lived under the protection of the British government, and who implored it, by every principle of mercy and justice. to remonstrate with the Rao. He stated, that his daughter, now seven months advanced in pregnancy, had been placed in strict confinement at Bhooj, and entreated that she should be removed from that city, and delivered over to his own protection; representing, as an additional reason for this measure, that two children, formerly born to Ladoba, had been put to death, on the plea of their being female, and that no other fate could be looked for to the expected infant and its unfortunate mother. Instructions were in consequence issued to Captain M'Murdo, to express to the Rao the deep regret of the British government, that so horrid a deed should have been committed at his court—an act which must, in some degree, reflect on the government which supported him by its friendship; to desire the punishment of the assassins; and to require, as the only means of atonement, his attention and regard to the widow and her expected offspring. Letters were at the sametime addressed to the Jharejah chiefs, intimating the expectation of the honourable the Governor in Council, that the widow and her child would be treated with kindness and respect, and requesting them to write to, and to visit the Rao, and to use their influence with him to secure so charitable a purpose.

This representation was viewed by Rao Bharmuljee with the greatest jealousy and distrust. He declared that the question was one entirely of a domestic nature, such as could admit of no foreign interference; and plainly intimated, that the further mention of it would lead to an open rupture. He immediately recalled his army from the Abbrassa, where it was still employed; augmented his troops in other quarters; and proceeded to make preparations of a nature quite at variance with the conduct of a friendly and pacific state. The question of demanding the restoration of Anjar on all sums being paid, was agitated in the durbar; and a plan was proposed to surprise that town, by introducing a body of armed men in a number of grass carts. The native British agent at Bhooj was treated in a manner little short of contempt; and every thing showed that the Rao wanted the ability, rather than the inclination, to proceed to open hostility.

The levies which had been collected were chiefly sent into Wagur, under the pretence of punishing the Khosas; but enough had been seen of the Rao's disposition, to induce the resident to call for reinforcements to the garrison of Anjar. A British regiment accordingly crossed the Runn from Guzerat; and application was made to the durbar for assistance in the way of supplies during its march. This request was not only refused, but the Rao ordered his troops under arms, prepared twenty-five pieces of field-artillery, and every arrangement was made to march, when the expedition was unexpectedly countermanded; the fumes of intoxication having evaporated, or his Highness having been deterred by the entreaty of some one remaining friend to his interests. On the approach of the battalion to Anjar, he stationed a body of troops ten miles in advance of Bhooj, and obstructed all communication between the two cities; but these were withdrawn a few days after on the remonstrance of the resident, and through the influence of Ruttunsi.

Meanwhile the conduct of Rao Bharmuljee appeared in a different light to the court of Hyderabad: and that extraordinary government, on hearing of the murder of Ladoba, sent an ambassador to Bhooj to *condole* with him on the death of his cousin ; to expatiate on the friendly disposition of the Ameers; and to offer him aid against any of the Jharejah chiefs who might prove refractory. Exaggerated reports had reached Sinde of the domestic disturbances in Cutch ; and their Highnesses, from a fear that the Rao would again request the assistance of the English, determined, if possible, to keep these, their constant object of dread, at a distance, by offering the necessary support themselves. The envoy was received, and treated with great respect ; but the durbar declined the assistance of the Ameers, purchased, as it is now believed it must have been, by the cession of the fortress of Luckput Bunder, on the eastern branch of the Indus, which, from its vicinity to their own frontier, had long been a desirable object of acquisition to the Sindians.

The Rao continued his reckless course of tyranny and dissipation. Excluding himself from the society of all except the dissolute companions of his pleasures, he was alike indifferent to the stings of conscience, and the sufferings of his subjects. A glimpse into the interior of the palace at this period is afforded by a letter which the widow of Ladoba contrived to send to her friends through the medium of a slave girl ; and in which she describes Rao Bharmuljee as having determined to violate her person, and murder her infant. The latter was saved through the entreaties of the minister Luckmadass, but the fate of the unfortunate mother has never been properly ascertained. Cutch was now fallen into as miserable a state as it had been in during the worst times of the mis-government of Rao Rahiden. Open rebellion and faction were only prevented by a dread of incurring the vengeance of the British Government, to which the Rao's hatred and dislike daily increased; and he was so infatuated, as to allow these feelings to evince themselves on every occasion. He never spoke of Captain M'Murdo but in terms of the grossest abuse; and, whenever intoxication supplied him with sufficient courage or candour, his designs against Anjar were loudly boasted of. His actions, moreover, in some measure, kept pace with his declarations. He put an end to the trade of the merchants of Anjar, by laying such duties on the cotton bought by them within his territories, as to render it impossible for them to send it to Toona; and, to complete the measure of folly, he prohibited vessels belonging to any other port from engaging in their service.

These aggressions were not permitted to proceed without remonstrance on the part of the resident. He had before taken various opportunities to entreat the Rao to discard his profligate habits and advisers. He now, with a degree of courage and decision equally creditable,—at a time, too, when every thing foreboded treachery, and when he had been privately apprized of intentions to murder him,—paid a visit to the capital, and personally warned Bharmuljee of the danger and folly of his conduct, and of its inevitable consequences. The particulars of Captain M'Murdo's interviews at the durbar have been related to me by the late Major Noble, an officer who accompanied him; and I have since been able to learn the real intentions of the Rao from persons then in his service. All accounts concur in stating, that he had given his consent to Tukkur Mohunjee for the assassination of the resident; and that it was only when that gentleman appeared in the durbar, that his resolution happily failed him, and the projected atrocity was countermanded. No respect, however, was shown to him or his suite on their visits to the durbar; on the contrary, they were jostled by the troops and attendants as they passed through the courts of the palace; their salutations were not even returned; and the populace appear to have been instructed, or, at all events, permitted, to assail them with ribaldry and abuse. The Rao himself was found intoxicated on every occasion of Captain M'Murdo's waiting upon him. He showed himself indifferent to every proposal which was made to him, and contented himself with flatly denying ever having given cause of offence. To a proposition to reduce the troops, agreeably to an article in the treaty, he turned a deaf ear; and the resident left Bhooj without having gained any one object.

Discontent and anarchy had now reached their height in this devoted province. Nutthoo Metha and others of the ministers fled, as the only means of saving their lives; and Luckmadass and his party became entirely favourable to the introduction of the British influence. The Rao's interference with Sandan, and an attempt he made to impose a tribute on the Jharejah chiefs as a body, gave great dissatisfaction to the Bhyauds, who addressed a letter to the Bombay government, in which they set forth, that they had never been in the habit of making pecuniary payments, and entreated assistance, in the event of the durbar's attempting to enforce its unjust claims; finally, they declared their conviction, that the interposition of British authority was absolutely necessary for a thorough reformation in the affairs of Cutch. The Bombay government did not consider itself called on to interfere in a quarrel between the Jharejahs and their sovereign, whose claim to the crown they themselves had so recently acknowledged; nor did it wish to take any decided measures till the Rao's conduct should be such as to render actual hostility inevitable. This soon occurred; for Bharmuljee, who had been daily becoming more and more infatuated, at length formed the resolution of attacking, by surprise, the town of Anjar, over some of the villages attached to which he had previously tried to assume an unwarrantable degree of authority. With this view, he summoned all persons holding lands of the durbar, by military tenure, including Meeanahs to Bhooj; and marched to Lackhoond with five thousand men, and eleven pieces of cannon. Before adopting this step, he had, partly by promises of future forbearance towards them, and partly by intimidation, induced several of the Jharejahs to accompany his army with their quotas of troops, or a portion of them.

The Rao attempted to disguise his real designs, by intimating to the resident his intention to move into Wagur to punish his refractory subjects in that province; though this pretence was of itself rendered glaringly improbable, from his having just previously recalled all his garrisons from that quarter. Preparations being made at Anjar to repel attack, he was forced to relinquish his views on that place, but he determined to adopt another mode of insulting the British government, and of showing his disregard of the treaty he had entered into. He suddenly marched against Arrysier, a town in the eastern extremity of Cutch, the chief of which was then residing at Anjar, under the protection of the resident, and engaged through his mediation in the amicable settlement of some disputes between himself and the durbar. Captain M'Murdo remonstrated in the most forcible manner with the Rao on the injustice of his conduct; reminded him that the Honourable Company had become, in virtue of the treaty, the mediator between him and the Wagur Zumeendars—that Killian Sing, the chief of Arrysier, had been called to Anjar, at his Highness's own request, to adjust all differences; and ended his communication in these words:—"Should you be determined in destroying Arrysier, be guided by your own pleasure; but in so doing, there will be no distinction from entirely throwing off all connexion with the British government."

This intimation passed unheeded by the Rao, who, contrary to every advice except that of Tukkur Mohunjee, and his confederates, continued to carry on the siege of Arrysier; and it was only after the expiration of two months, when he found that fort likely to baffle all his attempts, that he again thought of adopting a conciliatory tone towards Captain M'Murdo. He then addressed a letter to that officer, filled with general expressions of friendship towards himself and his government, without referring in any way to the communications made to him regarding his late proceedings; but this step, could it at any time have been effectual, was now too late: for the treaty between the governments had in the interim been suspended; and the Marquis of Hastings had proclaimed Rao Bharmuljee a public enemy, and had given instructions to proceed to the extremity of war against him. The object of his Lordship had been to effect the establishment of a government in Cutch, disposed to maintain the relations with the British power in India, fixed by the treaty of 1816; and as it was hopeless to expect this from a prince of Rao Bharmuljee's character and conduct, orders were issued to accept the spontaneous and long proffered co-operation of the Jharejahs for his dethronement, as well as to request that body of noblemen to elevate to the musnud whomsoever they considered the lawful heir to that dignity. To give full effect to these instructions, a British army was forthwith assembled, under the command of Sir William Grant Keir, at Anjar, where it was joined by Visrajee, the two Pragjees, Allyajee, and Myaminyee, the five principal Jharejah chiefs in Cutch, who expressed their readiness and anxiety to co-operate in the measures to be adopted.

The Rao, who had during this interval entered into a compromise with the chief of Arrysier, quickly returned to Bhooj, where he was seized with a violent illness. He was consequently unable himself to make any preparations, or give orders in person; but his partizans and favourites collected a considerable force; and on the approach of the British army to the capital, some skirmishing took place. Captain M'Murdo then intimated to Bharmuljee the intention of his government to organize anew the affairs of Cutch in concert with the Jharejah Bhyaud; and called on him either to stand by the consequences of resistance, or to surrender himself; promising, in the event of his adopting the latter alternative, that he should meet with safety and consideration. This proposal was not attended to till the Hill-Fort of Bhoorjeeah, which overlooks the city of Bhooj, was taken by escalade on the following day; upon which, through the negociation of the minister, Luckmadass, Rao Bharmuljee was brought to the tent of the resident, and placed under a guard of British troops. Every respect was paid to him, consistently with the safety of his person, and the kindest attention shown to his health, which, from constant intemperance, and his recent indisposition, was now so completely broken, that he was scarcely able to walk or articulate.

A few days after his surrender, Rao Bharmuljee was formally deposed, and placed in a palace built by Futteh Mahommed, which was selected for his residence. The Jharejah chiefs were then left entirely to themselves to choose his successor; and it was generally expected that the election would have been in favour of the infant son of the murdered Prince Ladoba; but, strange as it may seem, after a perusal of these pages, the only son of Bharmuljee, a child of three years of age, received the unanimous votes of the Bhyaud, and was accordingly raised to the throne by the name of Rao Dessul. The minister, Luckmadass, is understood to have secured, by his influence, this decision in favour of the offspring of his fallen master; an act of disinterestedness and forgiveness of injuries, which is highly creditable, when it is recollected that his own life was often in imminent danger from the violence and cruelty of the Rao, and that his property had been seized by the orders of that now unhappy prince. But Luckmadass, and many others with whom I have conversed on this topic, appear even then to have viewed Bharmuljee rather as the weak and infatuated minion of a base and profligate party, from which it was impossible to detach him, than as a man by nature cruel and tyrannical; and the minister's hostility against him seems to have been much softened at the crisis of his fall. Necessary as was his dethronement, several of the Jharejahs, acting from the same impression, still wished, after that decided step, that the government should be carried on in his name; and when they found that the proposal was objected to, they evinced their respect for his feelings and misfortunes, by entreating that kindness should be shown him in his confinement, and that the succession should remain in his family. The election of the Bhyaud proved in the end more fortunate than if it had fallen on the weakly child of Ladoba, (whom, however, they declared the next heir to Dessuljee, in the event of his not living to have issue,) as he died a few weeks after, and the race of Bhyjee Bawa, the legitimate branch of the royal family of Cutch, became extinct.

The next requisite step towards the settlement of affairs, was the appointment of a regency, to carry on the government during the minority of his Highness Rao Dessul; and the Jharejahs were again requested to nominate a sufficient number of persons for the purpose. Their choice fell on Jharejahs Visrajee of Roha, and Petrajee of Nangurcha, the two most powerful chiefs in Cutch, Oodowjee, a Rajgoor Brahmin, the minister Luckmadass, and Ruttunsi Jetta. The name of the British resident was also included; but as the object of the Governor-General was to render Cutch, as far as possible, an independent state, the arrangement was at first objected to; and it was only through the earnest solicitations of the Jharejah Bhyaud, combined with those of the existing members of the regency, that his lordship at length consented to the appointment of Captain M'Murdo as president of the latter body.

The measures which had been adopted at Bhooj gave satisfaction generally to all classes throughout the country; and no town evinced any unwillingness to acknowledge the new Rao and the authority of the regency, except Luckput Bunder, which was garrisoned by Arabs, of whose submission doubts were for some time entertained, but it finally surrendered without any military operations being undertaken against it. Matters being now settled on a firm basis, the regency proceeded to correct the innumerable abuses in every department of the state, and to discharge the useless and expensive levies of troops which Bharmuljee had maintained. A British force was subsidized for the defence of the country and the support of the government; and the honour of guarding the Rao's palace was given up entirely to the Jharejahs, to the exclusion of the low-born wretches whom the late Rao had introduced to that responsible duty.

The tyranny and injustice of Rao Bharmuljee had scarcely been crushed, and a new and better order of things introduced through the means of the British government, when the hand of Providence seemed to join in depriving Cutch of some of the instruments of cruelty. A violent shock of an earthquake, attended with some extraordinary circumstances, levelled with the dust nearly all the walled towns in the country, and anticipated an intention, which had often been conceived, of dismantling some of these nests of discontent and treason. The desolation which ensued can scarcely be imagined. In Bhooj alone, seven thousand houses were rent to their foundations, and twelve hundred persons buried in the ruins. Anjar suffered equally in proportion, and much injury was sustained, with the loss of many lives, at Mandavie and other large towns. The phenomena which accompanied this awful visitation, it is unnecessary to detail here, as they have been described in the Transactions of the Literary Society of Bombay.

In conformity with the spirit of the measures which have been detailed in these pages, and, as better calculated to maintain a firm and honourable alliance between the two states, a new treaty, containing, in addition to most of the articles of that of 1816, many others adapted to the improved condition of affairs, was shortly after concluded between the governments. It will be seen, on a reference to it, that the British government wished carefully to abstain from all interference in the Rao's internal authority; whilst it agreed to guarantee his power and the "integrity of his dominions" from all enemies, foreign and domestic. A bond of a similar description was extended to the Jharejah chiefs, who had established a claim on us by their conduct during the late revolution, and whose possessions were also secured to them, on their consenting to preserve their female children. In return for these important concessions, the advantages derived by the British government are almost nominal; for, with the exception of an annual subsidy of two lacs and eighty thousand rupees, equal to the support of one-half of the force which has been generally required, we receive nothing from the Bhooj durbar, to which Anjar and its dependencies have since been restored. In enumerating the benefits of the alliance, we must not omit, however, the grand victory in favour of humanity, in the abolition of infanticide; a horrid practice, which it has been our object, ever since our connexion with Cutch and Kattiwar, to put a stop to, and which we have certainly succeeded in diminishing in these countries.

If we take into consideration the dreadful state of affairs, which had existed for years before we entered Cutch, we must conclude, that the new arrangements were entirely in favour of that kingdom; for had not the British government interfered, and the strong arm of power, in this instance upheld by justice, been stretched out to rescue that unhappy country from confusion and anarchy, it must soon have ceased to be a state; and it would either have fallen into the iron grasp of the military despots of Sinde, or, if these had been excluded, Cutch would have become a prey, as before, to its own numerous petty tyrants. Indeed, it is impossible to conceive in what excesses the profligacy and imbecility of the government, and, we may add, the general depravity of the people of this wretched province, with whom bloodshed and treason had become as "household words," might have ended.

Postscript, 15th June 1829.—Since the period at which our narration closes, Cutch has continued to enjoy all the blessings of English rule. Disturbance has at intervals existed, but when serious, it has always been the result of famine, or causes of a similar nature, which no human government could control. The rains of 1823 and 1824 failed entirely, and the misery which this occasioned in a country solely dependent on the heavens for water may be conceived. Many of the inhabitants emigrated into Guzerat, and returned after the season of scarcity was over: while others less peaceable, crossed into Parkhur and Sinde, where, combining with military mercenaries from these countries, and adventurers from the neighbouring provinces, they formed themselves into bands, and made incursions into Cutch, several of the villages of which they plundered and destroyed. The more favourable season of 1825, together with the new and less oppressive system in the collection of the Rao's revenue, which was at that time introduced by the request of the regency, under the superintendence of the assistant resident, had the effect of putting an end to the outrages of these plunderers; most of whom had been forced by hunger to adopt their lawless proceedings, and on the re-appearance of plenty returned quietly to their native fields, which, with a few exceptions, the lenity of the durbar allowed them to retain unmolested.

The protection afforded to these lawless depredators, and to others of the same description, in the territories of the Sinde government, has brought us at different times into collision with the Ameers; and we have been forced on two occasions (1820 and 1825,) to assemble large bodies of troops in Cutch, in order to awe these chiefs into a maintenance of their treaties. By a new agreement concluded between the British and Cutch governments in 1822, Anjar and its dependencies were restored to the Rao, on his consenting to pay to us yearly the estimated revenue, viz. eighty-eight thousand rupees; making the entire sum we annually receive from his Highness to amount to two lacs, eighty-eight thousand rupees. From the famine which has been mentioned and other causes, this subsidy has been frequently ill paid, sometimes even remitted, and altogether has proved totally inadequate to support the heavy expences which have been entailed on us by our connexion with Cutch. Our government, it is true, have gained this province as a frontier; but its advantages in that respect are even doubtful; while, from its being a constant and unsatisfactory drain on our finances, the evils arising from the alliance have been great and positive. On this subject, however, it becomes not me to enlarge.

Of the persons alluded to in the foregoing narrative, some further mention may be interesting. Captain M'Murdo died soon after the treaty of 1819 was concluded,—much too soon for his country, and to the regret equally of the European and native community in Cutch, of which province he was the deliverer. He expired, and was buried at Burrunwao, near Palanswa, in Wagur, where his tomb is carefully protected by the inhabitants, and is an object of veneration, to which persons still make pilgrimages from a distance. Surely an amiable man need seek no higher reward than this for his exertions. His Highness Rao Dessul has now attained the age of thirteen years, and promises to fulfil the expectations of his subjects to the utmost. He has acquired a knowledge of the English language, from the instructions of the Reverend Mr. Gray, the chaplain at Bhooj, who has also instilled into his youthful mind a taste for astronomy and some other sciences.

His father, the Ex-Rao Bharmuljee, still continues a prisoner. The unhappy man has not yet attained the age of thirty-four, after having passed ten years of his life in confinement. When I first saw him, five years ago, he was a squalid miserable wretch, still in Futteh Mahommed's palace; and, from the period of his dethronement up to that time, had never been allowed to see his son, nor, I believe, any of the members of his family. Colonel Pottinger, however, who came to Bhooj as resident in 1825, and who, to the credit of his feelings,

> "Pitied child and parent separated
> By the stern mandate of unfeeling law,"

determined to ameliorate his condition, and obtained the sanction of government for his removal to a more comfortable residence. Since then he has occupied capacious apartments, elegantly fitted up, in his son's palace; where, though still under a guard of British troops, he is allowed every liberty consistently with his safe custody He is even permitted to go out twice a-week, when he chooses to take an airing, accompanied by a European officer and a few Sepahis.* His time is chiefly passed in the society of his son, the present Rao, in whose lessons he takes great interest, and for whom he entertains the strongest personal attachment. In the placid and dignified deportment of this unfortunate prince, none could now recognize the treacherous murderer, and the cruel despot who inflicted such accumulated miseries on his subjects. He is temperate, even to a degree; and his contrition, for the murder of his cousin, is believed to be heartfelt and sincere. It has, however, evidently affected his conscience frequently; and, with the view of atoning for his crime, he, in the year 1827, sent the ashes of Ladoba, at a great expense, under the charge of a body of Brahmins, to the holy city of Benares, to be consigned, with appropriate ceremonies, to the waters of the Ganges. Such are the uses of adversity, which has not failed to exert its chastening effect upon Rao Bharmuljee. I should not omit to mention, that the remains of Rao Rahiden have also been lately transferred to the same sacred city, to expiate his apostacy from the faith of his forefathers, and the many horrors which, as a Mahommedan enthusiast, he brought upon his country.

Kesser Byhee, the sister of Rao Bharmuljee, was eventually married to the Nawaub of Joonaghur, in Kattiwar, at whose court she died, it is

* Sir John Malcolm, on his visit to Bhooj in March 1830, at the request of the native government, ordered the guard to be entirely removed from the Ex-Rao Bharmuljee.

said, by unfair means. The natives of Cutch have a story, that her death was occasioned by poison inserted into her slippers. On the con clusion of the first treaty, Mahommed Meyan Sotah, and Sewiraj Hunsraj, who were obliged to disgorge immense sums of money which they had appropriated to their own use, fell into insignificance. They both died about the middle of the year 1818, it was supposed by poison. Hussain Meyan still lingers out a disreputable existence. He pays an annual visit to Bhooj, the scene of his father's greatness, and his own dishonour; while his gross and bloated appearance denotes the nature of his pursuits. Futteh Mahommed had some other sons, but none of them are known in Cutch. His daughter, whose person Rao Bharmuljee violated, has sunk to the lowest state of prostitution.

After the treaty of 1819, the affairs of Cutch fell chiefly to be managed by the British resident, the minister Luckmadass, and Ruttunsi Jetta, the Jharejah members of the regency declining, for the most part, to interfere. The most important of the latter, Visrajee of Roha, was detected in treasonable communication with some rebels in 1825, and was expelled from the administration, and banished from the capital; another chief being elected in his stead. His expulsion was followed in 1827 by the disgrace of Ruttunsi, who was found to be a defaulter to the state, as well as implicated in several mean and dishonourable transactions, which in the end overwhelmed himself and the whole family of Soonderjee Seojee in ruin, and lost them the esteem and confidence of the British government. Rao Dessul begins to show an interest in public affairs, and frequently holds durbars; but the chief management remains as yet in the hands of the resident and Luckmadass; and although the latter was believed formerly to be an actor in some of the melancholy scenes we have described, it is but justice to say, that his conduct now is marked by integrity. I may add, that he is the only individual at present in Cutch, who, from his birth and general respectability, is entitled to the elevation he has attained.